Angel in Your Mirror

Musings from the Curly Mind
of
JB Shelton-Spurr

© 2012 JB Shelton-Spurr
Spurr-of-the-Moment Publishing
Oxford, North Carolina
jbshelton.com
ISBN: 9780988252608

Dedicated to

Harvey Spurr, my husband

Cathy, Debbie, Deborah, Emma, Flo, Julie, Kim, King, Linda, Lois, Marc, Mom, Pat, Regina, Rosalie, Sharon, Susan and Waltye

With love, appreciation and Cheshire Cat grins

JB Shelton-Spurr

A collection of humorous and poignant essays by a journalist and rancher who delights in writing about children growing up and grownups reinventing themselves.

Acknowledgments

Versions of my essays
have appeared in
Carolina Parent
Christian Science Monitor
Herald Sun, Durham, NC
News & Observer, Raleigh, NC
Oxford Public Ledger, Oxford, NC
Washington Times

Used with permission

Table of Musings

Table of Musings moreso

1 Angel in Your Mirror

*Ghosts of Christmases past whisper gentle reminders. Gifts
-- given and gotten -- are all too often temporary
aberrations, quickly tucked away and forgotten, the gaudily
wrapped results of frenzied shopping.*

Surely the true Christmas spirit goes beyond searching for
the perfect electronic gizmo. Perhaps there is a better way to
celebrate the season.

Consider the friends and family members on your lengthy
Christmas shopping list. Select the folks who are the most
difficult and frustrating to shop for because (truth be told)
they have everything they need and little desire for the
unnecessary trinkets you compulsively package.

Tell the folks you know and love that you'll be presenting
gifts to young'uns you don't know at all. Have never met.
Wouldn't recognize if you saw them sitting on Santa's lap.

Their school photos aren't professionally framed and
displayed on your mantelpiece, documenting their smiling
faces, picturing their growth in self-confidence and maturity.

You won't be celebrating their report card successes,
attending their PTA meetings, and staying up late co-
creating their science fair projects.

Unlike your own children's hopes, dreams and desires, most
everything they wish for in life will remain a mystery to you.

Everything but a need for basic clothing necessities to keep
them warm. To give them that proud sense of going back to
school after Christmas break wearing an outfit nobody else
has ever worn. To glance in a mirror and smile at their
newly garbed reflection.

Your shopping mission will be easy: Warm a child's body and your own heart. All you need to do is visit a Salvation Army Angel Tree. The little you know about these youngsters is limited to an Angel Tree card that reveals each child's first name, age, gender and clothing sizes.

Choose a child's card (yes, you're welcome to choose more than one) and a curious feeling will surround and embrace you. It's simply the magic of the real feeling of Christmas.

Select the dresses and slacks, shoes and sweaters, shirts and gloves for someone special who deserves a gift-filled holiday in two ways.

First, the gift of items of clothing neatly folded into brightly wrapped, ribboned and bowed boxes, their reindeer-and-elf motif paper inviting the girl or boy to glance joyfully at the decorative outside before enjoying the contents.

Second, the gift of knowing that someone cared enough to select the Angel Tree card with his or her name on it, braved the holiday crowds, and bought clothing with thought, care and love. Consider tucking a toy or trinket into the gift box.

Bring your wrapped gifts back to the Angel Tree in time for the Salvation Army volunteers to accompany Santa on his sleigh riding, chimney sliding, and milk and cookie feasting.

Love isn't a word to use flippantly, especially about young'uns you don't know. But love is a most appropriate word to use when you play such an important role with a giving heart.

This year, if you're looking for an angel, go first to the Angel Tree, then to your mirror.

2 *Aunt Bee of Mayberry Wanted*

A classified ad to find the person I desperately need to help me get through life.

AUNT BEE WANTED

Seeking Renaissance woman who adores cooking, cleaning, keeping house, sewing, ironing, gardening, shopping for groceries and handling the myriad semi-rewarding details of running a home.

Prefer forgiving nature, with patience of several saints.

Roles include mother, friend, sister, aunt, nurse, comforter in times of stress, celebrant for occasions of joy.

Family-oriented, experienced sitter for babies, kids, teens, pets and husbands.

Abilities as confidante, motivational speaker, purveyor of common sense and humorist -- who helps me take life less seriously -- a definite plus.

Confident in negotiating with repairmen, door-to-door evangelists and Halloween trick-or-treaters.

Media personality willing to give up the glamour of her very own television cooking show to focus on her loved ones.

Tendency toward being a bit excitable and over-reactive, showing a sufficient number of foibles and fiascoes to reassure me that since you're not perfect, neither must I be.

Provider of warm, welcome home, listening ear, cookies and milk, and a closed mouth when I don't want advice, no matter how much I really need it. And will be there for me later when I'm willing to listen.

Salary: Negotiable. But if you're the right person, no one on earth could afford to pay you all you're worth.
Apply: Quickly, please, oh please, quickly!

Aunt Bee, I know the times they are a changin'. Just because you're an imaginary character on TV show reruns has no effect whatsoever on my thinking of you as a real person.

When you declared, "I want a big moment in my life, and I'm going to have one," you inspired -- and continue to perpetually in syndication -- viewers young and old.

You took those flying lessons, despite the discouraging manner of Mayberry's sheriff and barber who thought you might get "raptures of the sky."

When you overcame your hesitation to pilot that plane, you did it by telling yourself what so many of us tell ourselves. "I'm not ready. I don't know what I am. I think I'm going for a walk." We treasure your basic way to solving problems and identify with your plight. All of us have felt unready.

But it was you, dear Aunt Bee, who was plucky, determined and courageous enough to fly that plane solo over town. You proved yourself to yourself, not to or for anyone else.

You listened not to the naysayers, but remember the words of your flight instructor, "You can't quit now. You've already flown further than Orville Wright."

I know I'm not alone in needing and wanting my own Aunt Bee. With any luck at all, someone will come up with a way to clone her.

3 *Baby Teeth: A Fairy Tale*

Seven-year-old Emma wiggled into her pajamas and out of her upper front left baby tooth. She knew the Tooth Fairy drill all too well, having lost two other teeth. Emma clutched the little pearl of a tooth in her fist and ran into her folks' room, lispily announcing, "I've lofst anosure thooth!" Mom responded with gentle hugs, assuring Emma, "If we listen together, we'll hear the Tooth Fairy winging her way over the roof."

Indeed they did. It was a windy day; the pine trees rustled a la Tinker Bell in their imaginations. Emma tucked the tooth into a heart-shaped Tooth Fairy pickup-box, slipped it under her pillow and drifted into dreamland. But not before she wrote a heartfelt note to the Tooth Fairy.

Dear Tooth Fairy,
This is my very best favrit (sic) tooth. Please oh please don't take my tooth to be a star in heaven.
Love, Your freind (sic),
Emma

The next morning, Emma was thrilled to discover two crisp dollar bills and her tooth in the little box, a smiley-face sticker proving the Tooth Fairy's visit. She smiled the toothy grin of a little girl with a big idea.

During the next month, she traveled the neighborhood sleepover circuit, Tooth Fairy box in her backpack, Cheshire Cat grin on her greedy lips. Each morning, she exclaimed to her friends, "I've lofst a thooth. Let's show it to your Mom!"

Each Mom, three besides her own, congratulated Emma and bestowed the traditional two dollars on behalf of the Tooth Fairy. She was eight dollars richer before Mom #5 figured out her scheme and reported the dear child to her Mom.

Emma confided in me that she doesn't believe in the Tooth Fairy. She does believe in her own salesmanship, albeit with a limited product line.

Her Mom began a heart-to-heart talk, snuggling her daughter on her lap. "Emma, what you did was wrong, wrong, very, very wrong." Emma's, "I know, I'm sorry," came with a gap-toothed grin that evoked her Mom's smile of relief. Emma grinned again, happy her secret had come to light.

Mom temporarily segued into a quick daydream about her first-grader's rites of passage into the real world. "Can you imagine," she whispered into Emma's ear, "a world without the Tooth Fairy, Santa Claus and the Easter Bunny? Might we be silly enough to think the ventriloquist talks for his dummy, when everyone knows it's the other way around? Would we unpack our bags and cancel our vacation plans to the end of the rainbow?"

But, despite the temptations, she wisely left such thoughts unsaid. Emma's Mom reassured herself that the proper motherly message must be, "The tooth, the truth and nothing but the tooth truth." For in her heart she knew Santa Claus, the Easter Bunny, talking ventriloquist's dummies and road trips to the rainbow's end were tender notions of Emma's earlier years of innocence.

Emma has promised to leave future baby teeth in their proper place, in the little box tucked under her pillow, without notes to the Tooth Fairy or plans for recycling tiny white souvenirs.

Let's cherish the happy ending to our Tooth Fairy Tale, literally out of the mouth of a babe.

4 *Conquering My Fears*

"We have nothing to fear," said Franklin Delano Roosevelt, "but fear itself." Balderdash! We have death and taxes and things that go bump in the night. We have suspicious strangers, incompetent car mechanics and unreasonable bosses. And the little things -- spiders, bad hair days, running out of orange juice.

It's funny, in that strange and curious way, what we're afraid of, and how much time, energy and concentration we foolishly spend on fearing that which will never happen. I've spent more time worrying about things that never did occur than I care to think about or admit to.

My fears are mundane. Nightmares of my hairstylist getting cut happy on my curly tresses. The suspiciously alive red Jello that wiggles toward me when I open the refrigerator door. Last-minute remembering that the party dress I planned to wear tonight is held captive in the dry-cleaner's locked shop. These are, I must confess, the impertinent little annoyances blown way beyond the petty proportions they deserve.

I am most curious about those things that do not frighten me, perhaps curious to discover a patttern of bravery with them within me. I am at heart a brave soul, a woman who frustrates other folks by becoming increasingly calm as situations get worse.

Relaxation-responding has allowed me to doze off while the dentist drilled. Friends needing a ride to the emergency room hear calm tones and comforting words when I rescue them.

I've learned to conquer many business fears with a trick of memory, recalling that earthshaking meeting, proposal or interview from long ago that turned out to be truly successful or eventually unimportant. Stage fright has never made me quiver; I've given 20-minute presentations off the top of my head with two minutes' notice. Contract negotiations are challenges of game playing that I attend in a spiffy black suit, carrying an attache case and possessing an attitude of confidence.

It is, I realize, experience that is providing such confidence. I'm amazed by how much easier things become after the first time.

My remaining career fears are not exaggerated fight-or-flight fantasies, but reality based. My computer crashing when I'm on deadline. A client downsizing out of business before his check clears. Holding a press conference and no reporters covering the event because a celebrity has come to town.

My Dad's motto has always been, "Everything's under control." It took me years to realize his calm, reasonable and clever reactions to whatever happens do, indeed, give him less fear and more control. Come to think of it, President Franklin Roosevelt had a similar point about fearing only fear itself. It is, after all, how we react to a prospective fear that will or won't turn our thoughts and stomachs upside down.

And it was his wife Eleanor who said, "no one can make you feel inferior without your consent." Now if I can just remember to replace the word inferior with the word fearful, I will be the brave soul I know I am. I vow to do so: Please join me.

5 Daddyman, Greatest Superhero

As he strives to be the perfect superhero, Jeremy finds that protecting humankind isn't easy, especially when his mom won't let him wear his Spiderman outfit to preschool.

At age three years, five months and one week (birthdays are a precise, pride-filled science to heroic young'uns), balancing on a fine line between fantasies and realities is challenging.

Vanquish villains. Trounce evildoers. Overpower bad guys. They're everywhere. Hiding in clothes closets behind the rain gear. Crouched under the collection of Legos in the toybox. Guest starring on Saturday morning television shows.

Between morning cereal and bedtime tuck-in, Jeremy saves the day. Every day. His honor is at stake, defeating invisible foes. His superhero garb varies from day to day, reflecting humankind's need for his protective energies and his mood when deciding to be Superman, Spiderman or Batman.

Humankind's needs are sometimes superseded by realities that even Jeremy the Superhero can't control. Superman's cape shrinks to un-heroic proportions in a hot water laundry incident. The muscles and shoulder pads to fill out Spiderman's contours and simulate a powerful physique are temporarily missing. His kid sister Rachel thinks a Batman mask makes a wonderful chewing device for teething relief.

As much as Jeremy loves performing acts of superheroism in the get-ups of media-hyped, movie-sequelled cartoon adventurers, his favorite superhero isn't honored by the public. Hollywood producers aren't negotiating rights to his life story. Fans don't worshipfully tweet about him.

In the tradition of Superman, Spiderman and Batman, we honor Jeremy's superhero: Daddyman. He has many of the attributes Jeremy admires in his macho role heroes.

Daddyman can fly. His assistant books airline tickets, he proudly walks past the metal detector, strides to the gate and boards a plane. Not only can he fly, but he can also bring home nifty souvenirs for Jeremy and Rachel's toy collections.

The Daddymanmobile provides excellent transportation for achieving vital missions -- driving to preschool, his office, the supermarket, soccer practice and birthday parties.

Daddyman can send and receive secret messages by holding his iPad skyward and accessing gmail.

YouTube videos featuring Daddyman appear on the same TV set that shows Superman reruns, Spiderman cartoons and Batman movie previews. Personal movies shot on his iPhone reveal his photogenic presence at family celebrations.

Daddyman can fix anything -- from a toy Batmobile's wobbly wheel to a son's broken heart when his soccer team loses.

Disguises fill Daddyman's bedroom closet. He wears a suit and tie as Businessman, a T-shirt and jeans revealing Funman, Husband, Relaxedman and Time-with-Kids-man.

Daddyman doesn't run out of energy or patience until the work is done, the games are played, the questions are answered, the superhero movies are watched over and over again, and the bedtime stories are read. An exhausted, sleep-deprived Daddyman is nonetheless our hero.

Happy Father's Day to all the Daddymen in our lives.

6 *Daylight Saving a la Shakespeare*

"But, soft! what light through yonder window breaks?" It is the east and Juliet needs her second cup of cappuccino before she can be civil to Romeo.

It is the morning after the night before Daylight Saving Time. You've paid homage by setting your electronic contraptions requiring such attention 60 minutes forward.

Your mind and body are discombobulated. The church bells chime: 11 a.m. services are about to begin. Every thought, muscle and nerve ending is still on 10 a.m. time.

And, here's the rub: Those Saturday night festivities that kept you celebrating far into the night, zapping your energy, loosening your libido, cut into hours of precious sleep.

Assuredly, you need guidance from above. Sadly, you're too sleepy to get to church on time. If only you could go back to sleep. "Perchance to dream" it's six months hence for the autumn reprieve of setting your timepieces back an hour.

"What's in a name?" That which we call Eastern Standard would bestow upon us the grace of 60 additional minutes.

We wouldn't suffer this awful feeling of being late or missing an appointment and really not knowing the time.

"Swearing or baying at the moon" will do you no good. Seven a.m. looks darkly and suspiciously like 6 a.m. You will have to double your efforts to concentrate on the "toils and troubles" of adjusting to the new timeframe.

Monday awaits. Career, carpooling, daycare. "The course of true love never did run smooth," but never less so than when two adults, running late to get ready for work, share a bathroom. "Romeo, Romeo, wherefore art" my car keys?

"The lady may be protesting too much," instead of carefully listening to her body rhythms as she adjusts to the new schedule. The gentleman, yawning over breakfast, upset about a minor matter, may "make much ado about nothing."

We are at some time "masters of our fates. The fault is not in our stars, but in ourselves." In forgetting to set the clock radio's dual alarms: first, gentle classical music; second, an earthshattering buzz. Or neglecting to pre-program the automatic coffeemaker to waft a deliciously awakening aroma and memories of caffeine's inspiring spirits.

In coming home from work too exhausted to relax and too stressed to get a good night's rest. Or trying to be everything to everyone and fitting 48 hours of activities into 24 hours -- and doing none of them as well as we'd like.

"There are more things in heaven and earth, than are dreamt of in our philosophy." Can you survive "rude awakenings of tomorrow and tomorrow and tomorrow," as you gradually catch up on lost sleep?

"Parting is such sweet sorrow," yet wishing friends a fond good night "till it be morrow" is a self-protective move. Shakespeare knew when to leave the pub if he planned to write a sonnet come early morn.

Beware of sleeping potions. They wreaked havoc on the marital bliss of a certain young couple from Verona.

7 *Ducks in a Row*

Long ago, when my grandparents were courting, the weather hereabouts was whispered of as sultry. The word lingers on the tongue, a bygone description of old-fashioned romanticism and smoldering passion.

Their ways of cooling off lingered on their tongues as well. Sipping lemonade made with actual lemons, bits of pulp, sweetened with real sugar. Sampling hand-churned, home-reciped ice cream. Indulging in juleps resplendent with garden-grown mint.

From the safety of my windows-shut-tightly, overly-air-conditioned office, I face the beautiful and the frustrating.

My wild-flowered and tiger-lilied yard. Rabbits (toting lettuce?) eyeing my tomato plants. And (much against my will) a harsh reality: the summer weather of then is the summer weather of now.

Breathing as a challenge. Thinking clearly as an impossibility. Concentrating on work as an absurdity.

Memaw and Papaw are long gone, and with them a certain simplicity about life that I crave.

I needed an image, an inspiration if you prefer, to recreate that comforting feeling of the simple life. Neither a mission nor a five-year plan. Nothing high-tech or high-falutin'.

Papaw would've said, "Time to get your ducks in a row." Pawpaw could get away with overusing this line which, in his time, hadn't reached cliché status.

Aha ! I needed ducks. And the ducks of nearby Shelley Lake would be perfect. I envisioned them awaiting my visit. And, doing it all while neatly positioned IN A ROW.

Under the respected leadership of the Chief Duck, they would line up neatly according to size. Ready to glide peacefully through the water glistening in the sunlight. Cooling themselves under the branches and shadows of the trees and shrubs encircling the lake.

I arrived at the Shelley Lake bridge, a ducky place to observe mallards. They quacked incessantly, excited about sharing their duck wisdom.

I tossed Cheerios. They competed for each 'o' as if they'd never before been offered a nutritious breakfast cereal named after a Londonesque farewell. The destiny of duck/person bonding ends, of course, when the person runs out of Cheerios.

Their duck heads bobbed feverishly for the last few circles of food, quacking each other out of the way, until the competition stopped and the water's surface became smooth.

I waited for them to form rows, to glide across the lake as sunset began, to inspire me with simple, focused beauty.

They paddled in circles. They came on shore and quacked at each other and at me. They did everything but trip over their little webbed feet. In Southern summers, not even ducks can keep themselves and their thoughts in neat rows. If they can't, what in the world makes me think I can?

8 *Gift of Reading*

As a volunteer reading tutor at a local elementary school, I worked with first-graders who had special learning needs. Their progress, enthusiasm and budding love of reading deserved to be rewarded, I thought. Gifts of books would be the perfect way for me to reiterate what I'd been telling them all school year: I'm very proud of you.

When I mentioned my plan to the classroom teacher, she smiled gently and said, "JB, it's enough that you spend your time and love on the kids. You don't really have to spend money on them as well. And, frankly, it's not fair to the other students."

But these were kids who had their own battles of the books, wars with learning words, and triumphs over simple sentence structure. Nothing the teacher said was going to transform me into the Christmas Grinch. If she frowned upon my gifts, then I would devise another plan.

When I left school that day, I treated myself to a whirlwind tour of the children's section at a nearby bookstore. I selected specific books, knowing which ones would individually interest and excite my kids.

I also knew that these books would be ones they could proudly read on their own, by themselves, without help.

At the end of our last tutoring session before their Christmas holiday, I brought out their books. Interestingly, their classmates didn't show a bit of envy, perhaps thinking holiday homework was involved.

No, I wasn't foolish enough to gift wrap the adventures and poetry, humor and history, fact and fiction.

These are not gifts, I carefully explained to my students. They are loans.

I told my kids that I trusted them with the books, just as I trusted them to do their homework assignments, to do their best in school, and to question me if they didn't understand what I was trying to teach them.

And they understood precisely what they were getting into when they agreed to my long-term loan plan. As we all promised, I'll be meeting my kids in our classroom at 2:45 in the afternoon on the day before Christmas vacation in the year 2110, 100 years after the loans were made.

To me, the real gift was knowing that whether you loan a child a book forever or give it to her outright, you and the youngster are taking part in magic called a love of reading.

9   *Heart of Reading*

All I ever need to know I learned from a kindergartener named Tim.

I entered Lacy Elementary School in Raleigh as a volunteer committed to teaching a youngster the fine art of reading. I had the confidence of coursework at Meredith College in child development, psychology and teaching reading.

Turns out I was ready, naive and about to get my well-deserved comeuppance from a youngster worldly-wise for his six years of experience. We learned together, beyond reading, about life's realities.

We met in the school's media center for one-to-one tutoring that teachers, psychologists and reading specialists deemed vital to Tim's academic success. On our first day together, I realized tutoring a rambunctious youngster would be a physical challenge before it became a scholarly one.

It was difficult to hold (much less read) a book and simultaneously run down the hallway after my student, find his hiding place (thank goodness for his loud giggling), and securely tuck his squirming body under one arm for transport back to the books.

I've told friends I grew up at Lacy. They assumed I attended elementary school there as a student. I grew up at Lacy because that's where Tim taught me some of life's most valuable lessons.

Lesson 1: Have a Sense of Priority. When you're proud of your first new pair of Nikes, do not patiently sit still with your feet hidden under the table. Run like heck. When captured, treasure the adult pursuer's admiring comments.

Lessson 2: Strive to be Happy and Willing to Work for the Joy You'll Feel. In our tutoring sessions, Tim taught me about taking life one letter at a time. I promised to play basketball with him whenever he aced his spelling test.

We looked mismatched on the schoolyard court. Tim in his Nikes and me in my high heels, dressed for my next business meeting. No meeting I'll ever attend will be as important as the joy on the face of a winning speller.

Lesson 3: Know When to be Your Own Best Friend. Tim realized he liked to read, write and draw. He penciled text and crayoned pictures, adding a personal dedication line before giving each story to a cherished teacher or friend. One fine day he did not add the dedication; I asked why. Tim responded, "Because it's mine. It's for me." You have to know when you need to create for yourself. Tim guided me through his elementary school years.

Flash forward: Tim, a rising eighth-grader, was playing a pickup game of basketball. He enjoyed sports as he enjoyed learning, determined, energetic, loving challenges. But on that day, his playing stopped, abruptly.

Tim, age 14, grabbed the ball, shouted to a teammate, and died of a heart attack. If you ever wonder whether it's worth your time tutoring a child, think of my friend Tim, whose too-short life was enriched, as was mine, as we learned together.

10 Home Sweet Nest

Sometimes it takes a birdbrain to put life into proper perspective. Who could be better than a robin or a wren, a finch or a cardinal, to give humans a bird's-eye view on life?

From initial homeownership through feathering one's nest, to handling the empty nest reality -- a step beyond the mere syndrome. Ah springtime, with its rituals of house hunting and home buying. Moving into the perfect new nest may absorb most of a family's nest egg.

Simplifying the process is as easy as taking a few lessons from our feathered friends -- a family of cardinals who know the cardinal rules for creating home-sweet-nest.

The housewarming party is being held at one of the myriad home and garden centers that have blossomed throughout our town. The cardinal family's nest is tucked away, in comfortable privacy, in a hanging basket overflowing with hot pink petunias. Privacy is essential, as any mom and dad raising infants knows. The petunias add a decorative touch, while preventing the curious gazes of onlookers.

The flowers had initially attracted the cardinals to the neighborhood. The birds were nonetheless adamant about selecting a nesting place with other essential features. High enough for safety. Easy to fly in and out of. Roomy enough for the young ones on the way.

Mom and dad cardinal take turns guarding the nest and flying to the local worm-and-insect mart for sustenance.

The traditional real estate agent's mantra applies: location times three. Near food supplies; away from kitty cats. And, when the kids are old enough, a close expanse of nearby sky for flying lessons.

The cardinal parents decided to build their nest without benefit of a real estate agent, attorney, landscape designer, heat pump specialist or home decorator. They were confident in their abilities to select a site, construct and decorate.

Strands of Christmas tree tinsel add quite an imaginative touch to the nest's leaves, grass and pine needles. Their home glistens with that instant message of pride in ownership. This place is ours. There's no other place quite like it. One might well envy feathered homeowners who require neither instincts nor intuitions about schools and traffic.

A protective bird enthusiast (surely a home and garden center staff member) neatly magic markered a sign on the petunia-filled basket: Birds Nesting -- Not For Sale. Having good, caring neighbors provides family comfort.

Home exists for ourselves and the people we love. Child psychology pundits speak of blessing our sons and daughters with roots and wings. In that structure we call home, we adults bestow upon our children the roots of security and tradition and, all too soon, the wings of self-confidence and independence. Giving both blessings is so difficult to do. Yet it is so easy to picture a petunia spreading its roots in rich soil and a young cardinal taking her first flight.

11 *Hop Springs Eternal*

Pardon me. I've lost an hour. Have you, by chance, come across it? Same thing seems to happen to me every year, just around this time. I go into annual deep denial.

Who among us really has time to look for a lost hour, much less to make up for the lost time, unaccomplished deeds and unachieved wonders?

Ah, wonders. I'm experiencing my version of *Alice's Adventures in Wonderland*, empathizing with both Alice and her nemesis, the White Rabbit.

Nemesis because the bunny did take part in her downfall, albeit in the literary and literal senses of falling down his rabbit hole.

Alice, as, "she found herself falling down what seemed to be a very deep well...had plenty of time as she went down to look about her and wonder what was going to happen next."

My life lacks the pros and cons of Alice's predicament. I'm thankful that I'm not falling down any wells or rabbit holes. But I'm simultaneously envious of her opportunity to leisurely contemplate -- and perhaps even make plans for -- what she wants to happen next.

We all share lives in which we get "curiouser and curiouser" about how in the world we'll ever get it all done -- and maybe even steal a moment or two just for ourselves. Falling down rabbit holes are not the only frustrations we face.

The White Rabbit, like so many of us facing life's pressures, was talking aloud to himself. Exclaiming, "Oh, dear! Oh, dear! I shall be too late!," the Rabbit took a watch out of his waistcoat pocket, looked at it, and then hurried on. In a modern version of *Alice's Adventures in Wonderland*, the Rabbit would rely on an iPad and Skype.

I like to think that he'd also have a bit of sympathy for us during our daylight-saving time dilemma. We face the pressures of fitting 24 hours worth of personal and professional activities into those precious little minutes that make up a normal day.

Today, we not only dare to subtract 60 of those minutes, but we also jar ourselves awake thinking it's later than we think. And it is. As the alarm chimes, our minds and bodies feel as if it's an hour earlier. Ah, memories of sweet yesterdays -- the good old days before time escaped our grasps.

Is it too early and dark to run about my neighborhood to produce my annual contribution to neighborly love and increased cavities by hiding Easter candy for the local young'uns to find?

Am I confusing the bona fide local rabbits hunting for food by hiding chocolate bunnies under blossoming azaleas, jelly beans 'neath the forsythia, marshmallow chicks in the pansy patches? Do I have time to sybaritically devour a chocolate cream-filled egg, or do I gulp it quickly and guiltily?

But if I don't have time today for spring cheer and Easter enthusiasm, when will I? I'd better hop to it.

12   *Life's a Dance*

The elegant woman is garbed in a backless black gown. Her hairstyle is reminiscent of Audrey Hepburn. She is a poised party animal springing forth to celebrate her birthday in the grand style of a dinner-dance with family and friends.

Her name is Julie. Her father looks at her with love, with pride, with disbelief. "Thirteen-year-old girls don't look like that," he whispers to a friend. "Yes, they do," she replies. He winces in response, knowing it too true, too soon.

Julie knows her facts of life. Her father is learning them. Learning the intricacies of growing up has never been easy for any teen. It never will be. Facing the realities of a daughter growing up has never been easy for any dad. It never will be.

Dad, dear dad, looks at his youngest daughter through the blurry vision of tearful sentiment and sees a woman/child. His sight is blurred as well by the confusion of memories -- of magical times so long ago. Or were they just moments past?

Julie walks toward him. He asks, hoping for insight into the perpetual meanderings of the teenage mind, "How do you feel?" She will, he assures himself, reveal vital clues about the state of her psyche.

"I feel taller, much taller. I'm wearing four-inch heels," she says, then whirls away into a crowd of friends, before he can ask for a less literal answer. Dad wants a glimpse of her heart and soul. She provides a fashion report.

Julie the woman/child disappears, briefly, surrounded by giggling friends.

Julie the child appears, briefly, in her father's mind's eye, a four-year-old in a ballerina's outfit, giggling about trick-or-treating for Halloween candy. A split second later, she reappears, cozily tucked into a padded parka, winging snow angels in the backyard.

Another second passes, and she's a pony-tailed moppet, dreaming of winning Wimbledon, grasping a tennis racquet that's almost as big as she is.

Julie reappears, a child/woman needing her father. She speaks softly to him, through her tears, about a friend who is missing from tonight's party. Her friend died long before his time. He is forever missing from her life, but never from her heart and memory.

Her father understands, as only he can. And comforts her, as only he can. He remembers comforting her through the bumps and bruises of her childhood. He takes comfort himself in his perpetual ability to provide fatherly solace.

They dance. Their movements are those of a loving daughter and father. The steps and turns move them forward, backward and in circles, replicating real life.

Listening to the music and the lyrics, they improvise to a country tune. "Life's a dance. We learn as we grow. Sometimes we lead. Sometimes we follow."

The music stops, but the rhythms of growing up dance on.

13 Lincoln Never Tweeted

Abraham Lincoln enters the fourth-grade classroom. Evan, half-score-old student, sports a beard, dons a top hat and garbs chin to ankle in his Dad's topcoat.

He is taking himself -- and his historic character -- very seriously, facial expression stoic, posture perfect, right hand securely clutching a pocketed note. His resemblance to Lincoln is realistic, respectful and just a bit amusing to his fellow students.

The President is about to give a book report based on the life of an intriguing character: Himself. Evan presidentially clears his throat, glances around the room, locking eyes with audience members, and -- with a dramatic touch -- reveals the envelope on which he's jotted his talking points.

It's all very Lincolnesque. Consider the story (historically revealed as purely anecdotal) of Lincoln riding on a train to Gettysburg, grabbing the first piece of convenient paper -- an envelope -- and writing what was to become one of our nation's most important speeches.

The Gettysburg Address, only 246 words (too long for tweet, alas), was delivered in a little over two minutes: To put this in proper perspective, that's less time than it takes Evan to give his book report. May we all join historians, perpetually thankful Lincoln never tweeted. Picture him grinning at the absurd idea of condensing worldly ideas in 140 characters.

Actually, Evan doesn't give a book report. He intones, "When I was a boy" and then (in that classroom, 149 years after Lincoln delivered the Gettysburg Address) Evan becomes Lincoln.

He talks about his life and times, growing up and facing realities, growing older and improving the realities of life for his countrymen and women. Evan doesn't -- not once -- break character. As he ends his story -- Lincoln's story -- he gently tips his top hat in an old-fashioned sign of well-being, bows and gallantly walks, head held high, from the front of the classroom to his seat.

Lincoln stated, "The world will little note, nor long remember what we say here." But Evan has proven the great man wrong. As long as fourth-graders still read and remember, share and respect Lincoln's words, strive to create a world where all men and women are created equal, the world will note and remember Lincoln's words.

The Lincoln hat and beard were souvenirs of Evan's Cub Scout trip to Gettysburg, Pennsylvania, where he adventured and learned about history where history ought to be adventured and learned, close up, in person, on site.

Since that trip, Evan has graduated from Cub to Scout. Lincoln would be proud.

14 *Magic of Learning*

"Sandra's seen a leprechaun, Eddie touched a troll. Laurie danced with witches once, Charlie found some goblins' gold. Donald heard a mermaid sing, Susy spied an elf. But all the magic I have known, I've had to make myself."

Quoting Shel Silverstein's poem titled *Magic* is a dandy way to celebrate the beginning of a bright, shiny, irrepressible new school term.

Shel's *Magic* is a wonderful introduction for youngsters -- elementary school age in particular -- faced with new people (from little folks their own size to teachers who look like giants from a kid's eye view), new faces to recognize and smile at, and new friends to recall in names and adventures.

Over the years, as a volunteer reading tutor and guest book reader, I've had the opportunity to share my love of reading and poetry with kids at Raleigh, NC, elementary schools.

I discovered the secret of teaching poetry is being sure the kids have fun, use their imaginations and be creative while learning. The real secret of success was never telling them it was a poetry class until it ended.

Poetry has a bad reputation. It was best to let them enjoy the poetic moments first and reveal the truth later.

So I'd write Shel's *Magic* on the board. The class would read it out loud (giggling and smiling) and draw pictures to beautify the words with shape and color.

I encouraged the kids to use the poem to jumpstart a creation of their own group poetic endeavor. They incorporated their names and contributed lines aloud about the pretend creatures and real people they played with and loved deeply.

And then we'd talk about the poem's final line and what it meant to them: "But all the magic I have known, I've had to make myself." I'd ask, "What is magic to you?" "Magic is being myself, only better," was one delicious response.

They had come to school wondering what their parts would be to play. Suddenly, they were pulling figurative rabbits out of imaginary magicians' hats.

Effortlessly, they knew their classmates' names and interests by heart. They had shared time and talents, creating a class poem that was warm and funny and rather (I'm proud to say) a tribute to Shel Silverstein.

"Oh, poems are yucky," disappeared as their descriptive phrase and attitude toward poetry. The genre suddenly had enormous potential for them to learn from, to enjoy, to share.

Among the other poems written by Shel, poems kids and the kid-in-me adore, is the one that begins, "I have a hot dog for a pet. The only kind my folkswould let. Me get." It's a super conversation about kid/parent relationships.

Amazing what a couple of little poems can do. They're just about...magical!

15 *Meaning What I Say*

Was it something I said?

Clearly it wasn't, because what I meant to communicate had nothing to do with what you understood as my message.

Is anybody out there listening to anyone but himself? I hope so. And I hope to find him quickly, just to absorb some of this frustrating non-communication. In the meantime, please join wth me in trying to keep certain non-listening folks off our backs and away from our phones.

There's the "deliberate misunderstander," the person who knows the right answer to his question before you have the chance to say a word. Life's decisions provide only two choices: his way and the wrong way.

Meet the blatant "my-mind-is-elsewhere" fellow," whose response to your job loss is, "Glad to hear it. Have a nice day."

Then there's the "hesitating speech patterner," who stops mid-word, mid-sentence and mid-thought, and somehow begins again precisely when you think it's your turn to talk. He is also known as the "opportunist" who accuses you of interrupting him.

There are a host of other non-listeners: the "adamantly curious fellow," who thinks that saying you're on deadline means he must ask, "What are you writing about ?"

The "requester" asks for advice, but never follows it.

Finally, the "exister" has no excitement or interest in his own life, but needs the details of yours to feel fulfilled.

As I continue what I hope is not a quixotic quest for good communication, I share these basic principals:

Self-censoring. Think before you speak. You don't have to say every thought that meanders through your mind. Consider the needs, wants and schedule of the other person.

Attention: Pay attention to his words. That, my dear, is why the other person uses particular words. He conveys meaning.

Questions: Ask questions if you don't comprehend what you're being told. Automatic affirmative headshaking will only lead to confusion.

Messages: Don't mix verbal and physical messages. What's the point of plastering on a news anchor smile through the economic terror stories of the day? Putting on your happy face sometimes means you are putting on a false one.

Remember this: Say what you mean; mean what you say.

I realize that effective communication can exist in a nonverbal fashion. It's a touch, look, wave, smile -- a feeling that mysteriously crosses the boundaries of human-to-human communcation. But, far more often, that isn't enough.

I won't try to read your mind if you don't try to read mine. Let's talk instead.

16 *Motivational Little Engine*

Before bars offered attitude adjustment hours designed for us to imbibe our way into happiness, minister Norman Vincent Peale wrote *The Power of Positive Thinking.* The philosopher William James said, "We can change our circumstances by a mere change of attitude," and *The Little Engine That Could* chugged, "I think I can, I think I can."

For those readers who don't mind me revealing the book's closing scene, the Little Engine did go over that mountain, meeting the challenge, chugging, "I thought I could, I thought I could."

Sometimes the biggest obstacle to motivating ourselves to happiness is right between our ears. We always find the time and energy to handle life's inevitable crises -- never too busy to attend a friend's funeral, rush a sick child to the hospital emergency room, wait for the tow truck to convey the car to the garage.

Then why, as logical thinking adults, do we stall and rationalize when finding the motivation to plan and grasp and act on things that will bring us joy?

We get caught up in getting things done, trapped in getting them over with, before we feel entitled to a moment to remember what makes us happy. And too often when that moment is available, we remain victims of the day as we lived it, too tired, angry or frustrated to focus on what we'd like to do for ourselves.

Our motivations come from within and without, from our own desires and other people's directions. Growing up is learning to let go of what doesn't work for each of us.

I'm looking for a day that ends with such a warm feeling that I'd like to relive those 24 hours because they contained satisfaction and smiles, genuine achievement and pleasure. Not necessarily anything major; just minor happy moments.

I can stop looking, because I know I have to decide what I want to relive and to create those moments, hone these skills, use those talents, cultivate these friends and travel those adventures. I have to do it all without guilt, explanation or defensiveness. Simply because they'll make my life better. Not a simple task.

Motivation has to overcome that basic human fear of the unknown called change. The status quo, with all its highs and lows, has the advantage of comfortable predictability. Fear of changing our lives carries with it procrastination and missed opportunities, creating our own misfortunes. Not changing is not necessarily the easy way.

We spend much of our lives trying to motivate others. We forget (or perhaps never learn) to motivate people and ourselves by simple reminders to experience the joys of achievements only we can choose to create as our uniquely individual selves.

Taking time for such motivating thoughts and actions has life-enhancing, time-effective, energy-producing results. It requires taking responsibility for our own happiness.

Who has time to do that? If you choose to, you do.

17 *Need a Little Christmas Right Now*

Visions of sugarplums are dancing before my eyes. Clearly, it's a response to the temperature-humidity index reaching a lovely 105 degrees. Television meteorologists are unanimous in their warnings. Being outside, unprotected from Mom Nature's vagaries, presents dangers of mind and body.

Protect thyself in an air-conditioned womb: Be it home, office or movie theater. Sip gallons of sweet tea. Venture into daylight wearing sunscreen, insect repellent and fabric bits.

Frankly, I'm tired of the weather folks' repetitive singsong. So tired that I'm willing to start a fund to ship them all off to the beach for the duration of this traditionally horrific Southern tradition called summer.

In exchange for a small contribution toward their travel expenses, all weather reporters will be replaced by cheery Christmas carolers holding goblets of chill eggnog, wearing T-shirts emblazoned: STILL HOT, STILL HUMID, MAY RAIN REAL HARD.

Forgive me. I'm not breathing very well right now. The lack of oxygen reaching my brain is but an allergy-induced seasonal aberration further confounded by air I can see and feel, but can't get into my lungs.

I could energize my Christmas spirit by starting to crochet personalized finery for my loved ones, writing my holiday letter, and taking photos for the family card.

But -- come to think of it -- I've never been remotely tempted to do any of those things. The memory of somebody else's holidays has crept into my heatstroked brain. Perhaps salvation lies in using a visualization technique, pretending I'm ensconced in a better time and place. Namely, Christmas.

The lyrics, "I need a little Christmas, right this very minute," chime merrily through my mind. I envision the joyous holiday spirits of friendship and camaraderie replacing the intemperate funk that pervades the land.

I tried singing *Frosty the Snowman* to self-induce a respite from today's traffic congestion. As I sat in my car, sleigh bells rang: I was listening. No, 'twas merely a tension headache causing a slight ringing in my ears.

Nonetheless, with perpetual optimism, I began humming, *Here Comes Santa Claus.* No, actually here comes one of those I'm-going-to-get-home-before-you-do drivers, cutting across two traffic lanes with nary a signal or thank you.
Retailers (unselfishly heightening my holiday spirits) are contributing to my Christmas mood. Cozily warm autumn fashions are on display. Card shops feature collectible tree ornaments. My first holiday mail order catalog has arrived.

I'm in the Christmas mood. If I start untangling my tree lights, I may get the job done by late December. If you'd like to join in my early holiday spirit, come by. It's the house with the candle in the window, sounds of carols on the spinet and the air conditioner on full blast.

18 Party Animal Confessions

I'm one of the lucky ones. A baby boomer who finds the intricacies of getting older nothing less than splendiferous. Fact is, I took time out of my harried schedule to have my midlife crisis. I remember thinking it would be best to get this over with, with minimum fuss.

So on a pleasant Wednesday morning last November, between 10:00 and 10:15 a.m., I maxed out my charge acccounts on the Home Shopping Network, ate every bit of chocolate in the house, and applied more makeup than all the Kardashians put together.

Thank you for asking...yes, indeed, I survived the crisis I felt obliged to have. The obligation was, frankly, based on midlife travails and tribulations featured on websites and blogs. I was identifying in a pervertedly jealous way with friends who'd had the courage to plunge into major life changes without wreaking total havoc on themselves.

And I was listening to the oh-so-sincere ramblings of best-selling therapist authors who advise the mildly wacko (yet amusingly enthusiastic folks) who form America's core group of talk show guests and reality show stars.

I knew society in general would not let me get away with getting older without experiencing my officially sanctioned midlife crisis. But I pulled it over on society with a technicality. No one said it had to be a particularly long midlife crisis. Fifteen minutes, I found, were quite sufficient.

Charged items can be canceled or returned. Overindulging in chocolate can be aerobically motivational. Industral strength face paint can be washed off.

My midlife crisis is now a mere historical note in the personal journal of my life. I realize aging joyfully means maintaining the proper attitude and avoiding contact with anyone in the throes of midlife self-examination.

All this explains why I spent my birthday with a friend who was born on the same day. In a slightly different year. OK, significantly different decade. My baby-booming birthday festivities will be remembered by my participation in my friend Angela's fifth birthday celebration.

Party animal that I am, I was flattered to receive an invitation to her birthday party. Thrilled, actually, even though I could total up the ages of everyone else on her guest list and still be a couple of candles short of lights on my own cake.

I've learned from experience that it is physically, mentally and emotionally impossible to suffer midlife angst while tunneling, bouncing and climbing amidst the brightly colored foam, fabric and structures of an indoor playspace. I found myself laughing unself-consciously amidst the antics of a group of partygoers who think of kindergarten as a place for folks older than themselves.

I cherish Angela's mom videotaping our shenanigans and saying, "I watched you and the kids playing and couldn't tell who was having more fun."

19 *Search for Security*

It senses and responds, gives comfort and support. Sounds like a perfect mate. Pity it's a mattress in a television commercial. I'd like to have the atttributes of that mattress at 7:00 a.m. when my iPod bursts into *Beethoven's Fifth* and life officially begins. It would give me a sense of security.

Linus strolls through the *Peanuts* comic strip gripping the security blanket that has given him cartoon life solace. Unlike Linus, if I had a security blanket to carry about with me, it would have what seamstresses call crazy-quilt patterns.

My bed covering would have been created by mixing scraps of clothing sewn, worn and outworn by lovingly remembered family members. My security blanket would reflect a charming historical tableau. Bits of lace and gingham for frivolity, denim and corduroy for strength, silk and satin for special occasions.

Let's be realistic. I would trade the memorable past -- pattern by pattern, design by design -- for a solidly colored and constructed blanket with SECURITY emblazoned across it lengthwise and a matching pillow case.

We all need a safe place to come home to. Safe in basic necessities and physical comforts: The proverbial roof above our heads. And we all need a safe place to come home to -- not just above our heads, but within them. That is the security of knowing our minds, respecting our thoughts, using our knowledge about ourselves to determine how to live our lives.

Letting go adds to that measure of security. It involves knowing when to allow ourselves the freedom, wisdom and delight of not continuing our lives as they are. It means decisive actions to escape our life traps and patterns, to give up habits, repetition and fear of change that hurt us.

Why do we spend our hours, energies and relationships in ways that don't fulfill our inner selves? What and how can we change? Do we take take time to consider new actions?

In another TV commercial, a husband and wife have invested their life savings to create their dream, a bed-and-breakfast to house travelers seeking their own solace, comfort and adventures. As their guests leave for the evening to wander through the beautiful village nearby, we hear the couple chant, "We'll leave the light on for you."

They've recited a warm and friendly message of security: You'll have a safe place to come home to. Our light will be a beacon to warn you of danger and guide you to safety.

I imagine the innkeepers have braved the insecurity of changing careers and challenged themselves to remain a happy couple while perpetually working together. Perhaps they've overcome self-doubts and financial difficulties and rarely question their new lives in a new place.

I pretend they are friends of mine, not characters who only exist between sitcoms. To dramatically drive the message of security home, watch the long camera shot as the commercial ends: The bed-and-breakfast is a converted lighthouse.

20   *Sex Defined*

Being a godmom is best done with love, not logic, especially when the godmom is a well-intentioned woman with no children of her own. I get goosebumps realizing I'll forever be Gabba, my goddaughter Emma's version of godmother.

I taught infant Emma about the birds and the bees, nestling her in my arms and carrying her around my backyard. I named the greens of leaves, the red chests of cardinals, and the baby blue skies filled with bunny and puppy clouds.

Years have disappeared in a magical, mystical haze. Emma is celebrating her sixth birthday. She is a kindergartner who adores learning and singing country music lyrics.

"Man, I feel like a woman!," my Shania Twain diva wannabe bellows, gyrating hips and tossing hair. "Gonna let it all hang out," she screams.

She's not a woman. She doesn't have anything that would hang out even if she wanted it to. If she feels like a woman as a kindergartner, I quiver thinking of her pre-pubescent years.

We are in the elegant ambiance of Lord & Taylor's children's clothing department. One of us (the younger one) is happily stripped to the waist. Little Mermaid panties are her only ode to modesty. She sings, "Go totally crazy, forget I'm a lady."

Emma is experienced in feeling like a kindergartner, a running-after-the-ice-cream-truck kid, a tearful Gabba-I-skinned-my-knee-and-it's-bleeding soulful little girl, needing a reassuring hug and a Cinderella bandage. How could she know what it feels like to be a woman and a lady?

Discouraged not a whit by her nervously giggling/cringing grownup audience, she belts out, "If you think I'm sexy!" Another song, another learning opportunity.

OK, Emma, calm down. Or am I telling myself to calm down? Surely she doesn't have a clue to what's she singing about. I ask, "What does sexy mean?"

"It means you look cute when you're naked," immediately responds little miss know-it-all. Too accurate, I dare to think, saying nothing aloud, my heart and head spinning.

She knows more than I want her to know, earlier in life than I'd like her to know it. Emma is still singing at the top of her lungs. Even if I had age-appropriate wisdom to share, she couldn't hear it, my Gabba-self rationalizes.

"Really go wild. Yeah, doin' it in style," miniature Shania wiggles on. She's a whirling dervish of personal style as we scan the racks for school clothes.

Even kindergarten has a dress code. No spaghetti strap tops, belly-button revealing T-shirts and jeans hanging off hips.

Emma runs around the Girls Sizes 4-7 section and chooses a size 5 T-shirt emblazoned *I'M A PRINCESS* and purple tie-dyed jeans with beaded fringe.

Add a Princess Ariel backpack and the look is perfect for the cover of *Kindergarten Fashions* magazine, if it existed. She's taught herself model poses worthy of a *Vogue* superstar.

It's going to be great fun watching her grow up into a woman and a lady. Fashion styles change. Godmom-goddaughter relationships are lifetime commitments of love.

21 *Songs in My Heart*

I perpetually have songs in my heart -- hummable hymns in my throat and improvisational jazz vocals a la Ella Fitzgerald on my lips. Alas, these locations no longer suffice.

Am I the only one who doesn't have 500 favorite songs on an electronic device the size of a pack of gum? Please tell me I'm not alone.

I must be iPod-ed, according to Emma, my beloved ten-year-old goddaughter and technology guru. She has a gleam in her eye and spouts attributes I hadn't considered. "Music is just the beginning," she says. "You can download videos, TV shows, audiobooks and podcasts." Oh, goody, podcasts. Note to self: Find out what a podcast is.

"And, Gabba (my godmom nickname), iPods are great for working out," she assures me. I wonder how picking up a five-ounce sliver of technology will help me get in shape. Oh, I'm supposed to take my song-enriched little buddy, plug myself in, and jog around the park, barely noticing my huffing and puffing thanks to distractions flooding my ears.

How in the world can I live without this contraption? I decide to lose my musical high-tech innocence and join the cheery band of entertainment aficionados who are literally plugged in and tunefully turned on at every moment. Does everyone else nod off into dreamland with iPod attached?

Farewell, oh faithful flock of sheep; you can no longer count on me, nor I on you. Insomnia be gone. Here's the new bedtime ritual: brush teeth, say prayers, and hook myself up to Mozart's *Eine Kleine Nachtmusik*.

Dear Emma, with a comforting solemnity, revealed, "When I was really little, I thought computers were filled with little-bitty scientists who never had to go to the bathroom."

Oh, I sarcastically tell myself, my iPod will be filled with teeny-tiny musicians with huge kidneys for their body size. Makes sense to me -- and provides as much detail as I want to know about how the device works.

To surprise Emma, I decided to make a fool of myself and continue my tendency to fake high-tech knowledge by bravely venturing into my local iPod-stocked retailer. My plan was to seek guidance from a salesperson who'd be gentle with me.

I found him. The fine young fellow was informative, patient, and a heck of a good salesman considering all the accessories I now own in addition to my hot-pink encased, two-gig toy.

Tony Bennett may have left his heart on the West Coast, but his dulcet tones join a plethora of entertaining mayhem within my grasp: symphonies by Bach and Beethoven; poignant country-and-western music; Broadway show tunes and all that jazz; NPR interviews. Podcasts are the next wave of my downloadable future.

Sure, you're impressed by my high-tech abilities. No need to be jealous. Emma did all the downloading, smiled her I-love-you-godmom grin, and convinced me to let her borrow my iPod for just a little while. She'll return it eventually, but until then, I'll be satisfied with the perpetual songs in my heart.

22 *Sunday in the Park*

Folks in my neighborhood speak a variety of languages.
Translation is never easy when cultures, histories and
passions collide.

But last Sunday, walking together on the trail around Shelley
Lake in Raleigh, we succeeded in communicating.

We were a quintet of contradictions. A preteen precociously
questioning. Older sister and brother spouting mysterious
teenage lingo. Grandma subtly voicing senior sophistication.
And me, their neighbor and scribbler of neighborhood events
for the local paper. I've finessed my way into this family as
friend, big sister and honorary second mom.

Our pre-walk warm-up session -- taking deep breaths,
jogging in place, flexing a bit -- evolved into a discovery of
genetic blessings. Without conferring, we simultaneously
stretched our arms toward the autumn sky, then bent over
and touched fingertips to toes. How proud we were of our
athletic prowess, or at least our ability to get upright again.

As it turns out, grandma and I share much in common.
We've both spent lifetimes watching, encouraging and loving
the kids.

Walking as a fivesome proved an impractical endeavor,
requiring jumps aside for bicyclists, in-line skaters and
oncoming strollers. So we formed conversational duos and
trios, rather like a party in motion, chatting for a while, then
rearranging into new groups.

At times, we each sought an alone-but-not-lonely contemplative segment of the trail, holding back a bit or scurrying ahead, but always rejoining the others before too long. We talked about our lives with caring and intimacy.

On a day when the leaves were beginning to turn richer colors, fall and crunch beneath our footsteps, when baby squirrels scooted across the road, when wildflowers blossomed without a touch of humankind's help, our priority became forming an admiration society for well-fed ducks.

We slogged through a muddy patch on the back trail, wending our way over slippery rocks, helping each other through soggy clay where the mushrooms mushroomed.

Each generation, we all realized, has its own points of reference -- people, events and experiences that require no explanation to those of a certain age, and are almost impossible to explain to those of another generation. It's difficult to celebrate, care about, laugh or cry for, what we don't understand.

Tony Bennett became our mutually beloved hero, a man we all connected with as a source of pleasure, whose song lyrics needed no translation. The mellifluous balladeer of love songs past has become non-generationally loved. We know we have more in common, more to share, than just Mr. Bennett. We have only to ask and listen. At times, not a word was spoken as we silently enjoy each other's company.

We realized the end of summer, the beginnng of fall, gave us a way to get in touch with the beginnings and ends of our individual evolving, as we mosey, skip and speed into life's next stage.

The best translations don't always come from mind or with voice. They come from our hearts.

23 *Wisdom of Winnie-the-Pooh*

A.A. Milne gave life to Christopher Robin Milne, twice. In real life, as his father. In literary life, as the author of *Winnie-the-Pooh* and *The House at Pooh Corner*.

He wrote about a little boy named Christopher Robin, who shared childhood adventures with Winnie-the-Pooh, Piglet, Eeyore, Tigger, Owl, Rabbit, Kanga and Roo.

Adventures that were read to us when we were children. Stories we shared with our children, who share them with our grandchildren. Our lives go on. So do the imaginary characters' lives. But let me tell you about the day the real-life Christopher Robin died.

The friends of Christopher Robin -- Pooh and you among them -- are invited to gather in the Hundred Acre Woods. To comfort one another, share memories, and say a peaceful goodbye. Shhhh...the memorial service is beginning. Open your book.

"Nobody knew why Christopher Robin was going away," wrote Milne. But they knew "Things were going to be different. They spoke with each other in such a hopeless sort of way that it really didn't seem any good waiting for the answer."

Piglet: "I think that I have just remembered something I forgot to do yesterday and shan't be able to do tomorrow." Piglet sidled up to Pooh from behind. "Pooh!," he whispered.

"Yes, Piglet?" "Nothing," said Piglet, taking Pooh's paw, "I just wanted to be sure of you." "But, Eeyore," said Pooh in distress, "what can we -- I mean, how shall we -- do you think if we...?" "Yes," said Eeyore. "One of those would be just the thing. Thank you, Pooh."

"And how are you?" said Pooh. Eeyore shook his head from side to side. "Not very how," he said. "I don't seem to have felt at all how for a long time. Piglet remembered he "wasn't afraid if he had Christopher Robin with him."

Pooh recollected that "as soon as he saw (Christopher Robin's) Big Boots, an Adventure was going to happen and he brushed the honey off his nose with the back of his paw and spruced himself up as well as he could, so as to look Ready for Anything."

Owl, who was wise in many ways, respected Christopher Robin, "who was the only one in the forest who could spell...he was one of those Clever Readers who can read things and who told us what messages meant."

"Oh! Piglet," said Pooh excitedly, "we had gone on an Expotition, all of us...to discover something."

"Something fierce?" Piglet had asked anxiously. "But if Christopher Robin was coming, I didn't mind anything."

Eeyore, by himself, in a quiet moment, wrote a poem, titled POEM: "Christopher Robin is going. At least I think he is...Do we care ? We do. Very much...All his friends send Our love."

"Pooh," as Christopher Robin had requested during the final conversation, "promise you won't forget about me, ever. Not even when I'm a hundred." Pooh thought for a little. "How old shall I be then?" "Ninety-nine." Pooh nodded, "I promise."

Pooh has asked me to tell you that if you forget the service is for Christopher Robin and think it might be for someone you loved and still love, it's all right to cry. He understands. And he has a box of tissues ready to share. I promise, too.

24 Young'uns Take Charge

PLEASE DO NOT LEAVE YOUR CHILDREN IN THE LOBBY WITHOUT SUPERVISION (a poignant plea emblazoned on the sign at my hair salon)

Children know and shout about it. Many adults know, but won't admit it out loud.

Truth is, at times we'd be better off if we adults weren't left in the lobby without children's supervision.

I am an adult. I'm pretty darn sure because it says so on my driver's license, voter registration card and credit card bills.

Spring fever has taken hold.

I'm thinking about the prospective pollen count, filing my income taxes, and cleaning (or selling, if that's easier) my house before friends with vacuuming fetishes visit.

But I'm also reminiscing about that classic childhood refrain: Spring is sprung, the grass is riz, I wonder where the birdies is.

I'm starting to realize my thought patterns are two squirrels short of a bird feeder.

Clearly, I am in desperate need (no, I don't feel alone in this) of supervision that only an expert under age 12 can provide. Supervision with a sense of humor. Without a need for perfection. With a refreshing innocence of uncensored honesty.

A friend who provides that joyous feeling expressed by Christopher Robin to Winnie the Poo, "As soon as I saw you, I knew an adventure was going to happen."

When I grow up (not a chance -- it's politely called perpetual childhood), I want to be like Julie. At age 11, she intrinsically knows how to supervise an adult. Be gentle in words. Be enthusiastic in deeds. Never forget that life is an adventure ready to begin.

She introduces me as myfriendJB as if it were a single word. She flatters me with the remark, "You're not like a real grownup at all." She dedicates a poem titled *JB is Jovial and Bursting with Happiness.*

She believes in me. She thinks I am exactly who I'd like to be. Who wouldn't want a "Julie" in her life ? Find your "Julie." Childbirth, a neighbor's daughter, tutoring a student are ways to do so.

Pay attention to her. We grownups have so much to learn about balancing work and play. If you are lucky, she will supervise you into enjoying life.

She has the infinite wisdom to know that catching fireflies, appearing in the school play, and visiting an art gallery are events to share and savor.

She will express her opinion in no uncertain terms, without playing grownup games. You will love her for this.

Invite Julie into your office. She will remind you that life is more than chamber of commerce meetings, contract negotiations and writing speeches. She will twirl in your leather swivel chair and giggle at your offer of a cup of coffee. She will decorate handcrafted Valentine's Day cards for all her classmates.

She will proudly present you with the business card she created on her computer. The card provides her name, address, phone number, email, and a job title that reveals she knows exactly what her job is: *Being a Kid.*

25 *Zach's Rabbit in the Hat*

Once upon a time I met a rabbit puppet who popped out of a magician's hat. My bunny encounter began when my friend Regina, a kindergarten teacher, invited me to read to her students. "JB," she said, "you'll love my kids and they'll love you. We'll all sit on our classroom carpet with its individual squares marked for each letter of the alphabet."

How could I resist the possibility of claiming the "J" square, surrounded by 23 kids wriggling, giggling and listening to me read from Regina's favorite book, *The Tale of Peter Rabbit.*

Not wanting to go empty-handed into the classroom, I stopped by a toy store, fell in love with a rabbit puppet and took him to school. He hid inside his black felt magician's hat until after story time, when I literally closed the book on Peter's adventures and wiggled my fingers inside his chapeau. Voila! Up popped a white-as-snow, grinning-up-to-his-giant-ears, fluffy, pink-nosed, bow-tie-wearing rabbit.

Then, much to the kids' surprise and delight, the rabbit asked, "Do you want to pretend you're a magician?" Although he sounded like me, the girls and boys didn't care. "I do," one said. "Me, too." "Me first."

To anyone but a seasoned teacher, getting a group of excited five and six year-olds to take turns is as challenging and confusing as getting real bunnies to behave. But Regina announced, "Let's take turns alphabetically by name." She quickly added, "But first, let's name the rabbit."

Several cries of "Peter. Let's call him Peter," resounded from the voters. Katie suggested Bunny-Bunny. When Zach shouted Rabbit in the Hat we had our winner.

"We'll take turns holding Rabbit in the Hat and pretending we're magicians," said Regina.

In an ironic turn of events, Zach's bottom covered the carpet's "A," so he went first. I showed him how to nestle his hand inside the puppet with his fingers moving to point and clap. Zach announced, "I am Zach the Magical. When I point the Rabbit at my Dad, he will become a rabbit, too." Fortunately, Zach's Dad wasn't in the room for us to test this trick.

Beth sat confidently upright. Rabbit on hand, she said, "I am Belinda, the Magic Girl. I fly around the world and make people smile." Each child became a magician. Yvonne of the "Y" square was last. She snuggled the Rabbit's pink nose on the cheeks of nearby classmates, and whispered, "I am Yvonne. Friends are magical."

"Thank JB for coming to our classroom and reading to us," said Regina. I heard a chorus of "Thank you, JB," as the kids surrounded me with a giant hug. Yvonne looked so sad when she gave me the puppet. In a voice similar to mine, he said, "I want to stay here and be magical with my new friends." I left, sans puppet, promising to come back soon.

Two weeks later, Regina's kindergartners invited me to an official ceremony and gave me a book titled *The Rabbit in the Hat,* filled it with crayoned artwork and magical ideas. I treasure the book to this day, along with a second rabbit puppet I bought and named Rabbit Hat Too.

He reminds me that magic for a child requires more than a puppet. It's magical for a child to know that he is among friends, including grownups happy to listen to his thoughts and dreams. Perhaps it's just my imagination, but Rabbit Hat Too has a very self-satisfied bunny grin on his furry face.

www.ingramcontent.com/pod-product-compliance
Lightning Source LLC
Chambersburg PA
CBHW061457170626
46811CB00004B/1548